SELF-LOVE

#MomfidentAF

JOURNAL

A Space For Mamas To Build Their Daily Self-Love And Gratitude Practice

Courtney St Croix

#MomfidentAF Self-Love Journal

Cover and interior design by Courtney St Croix
Photography by Hilary Spencer

ISBN: **978-1-9993857-1-2**

For more information, visit www.GetMomfidentAF.com,
find @MomfidentAF on Instagram, or email hello@MomfidentAF.com

hi!

Hilary Spencer Photography

hey girl, hey.

If you've picked up this journal, it means that you want to *do better*. It means you want to build a more loving, happy and confident sense of self; it means you want to feel better about your body and your self-image, and create a mind full of acceptance, self-love, gratitude, and positivity. It means that we have these values in common, and I think it also means that we just became best friends. All-right! *wink*

I get it. Living the modern mama / woman's life is hard. It's hard not to doubt, criticize and judge ourselves, our abilities, and our appearance when we're constantly comparing our real lives with the false-perfection of media—the fake, photoshopped and edited "squares" that always seem to be shouting at us to look a certain way, making us feel inferior or unworthy if we don't. We consciously and sub-consciously feel like we could never *possibly* be "good enough", "smart enough", "pretty enough", "successful enough", "happy enough", or "enough" of a mother, sister, friend, colleague, and every other role we play. I get it.

I have been working hard for a long time to create the kind of self-acceptance and confidence that makes me feel unstoppable, and one of the most influential components to making giant shifts in my own personal life has been journaling—writing down my roadblocks, overcoming them, putting thoughts into perspective, and then hashing out my feelings about a struggle or a success. It has been probably the most important factor in my growth as a good, self-assured and confident mom and human over the past four years. And so instead of writing sans structure in my regular old blank notebook, I thought I'd make my own journal and that maybe someone else might enjoy a quarterly journaling experience where they can reflect on their day, create a gratitude routine that sticks, and have a keepsake of different periods of our lives through writing that is therapeutic and cathartic all at the same time.

If you've picked up this journal, I know you're "into it" and will likely LOVE putting pen to paper and keeping this baby by your bedside, in your purse, alongside your agenda or even on your desk at the office.
OKAY, SO, HOW DO I USE THIS JOURNAL?

"Coles" notes: it can be used any way you damn well please. This is YOUR journal, use it as you see fit! If you need more direction and explanation, keep reading. The journal was created to be used ,for three months as a "challenge" of sorts that you can try out and note down any substantial differences in your attitude towards yourself and your life.

But here's the thing: I know this is challenging, because a) creating a new habit around journaling is hard, especially if it's new to you, and b) it's also a bit intense to start a strict MUST-DO-EVERY-DAY practice when the feeling of failure that you might subsequently "ruin it" by missing one freaking day is looming around the corner.

So girlfriend, you can start out with one great week, and then miss three days and start again. No big deal. The pages are undated on purpose, so you can just aim for every day, and if that doesn't always happen, you'll still have three-month's worth of awesome gratitude evidence, even if it takes you eight months to actually fill 90 days of pages. You do you, girl.

The bottom line is, the journal was created to help foster a stronger sense of gratitude and self-love for your life, self, mind, and body, in whatever stage you are in <u>RIGHT NOW;</u> not to stress you out because you can't perfectly do 90 consecutive days of gratitude, then make you feel bad about it. Nah, girl.

I hope you have fun with this book and use it like a companion to set the theme of your days in the coming weeks and months. I hope you learn a little about yourself, are able to enjoy the challenge, and will see a great improvement in your overall life-view by the time you hit 90 days of focusing on it.

Reach me anytime at GetMomfidentAF.com or on Instagram @momfidentAF if you have any questions, and I'd be happy to offer my advice and suggestions as you travel along your own self-love path.

With love, respect, understanding and gratitude,

Courtney

Step 1: Create Your Self-Love Vision

What do you <u>want</u>?

If everything were perfect in your life TOMORROW, if you accepted yoursef, your body, and started every day from a place of complete self-love, what would that mean? How would you feel? What does self-love look like to you? What do you want your default self-talk to say to you?

Write down your self-love vision. The way that you'd like to feel about yourself, if you never had any doubts, negative self-talk, criticism or judgement again.

Pick words, phrases, or descriptions that reflect that "perfect world" feeling of self-love. <u>Then, dog-ear this page, and look at it every day before you start journalling.</u>

This is your Self-Love Vision.

MY SELF-LOVE
VISION

Step 2: Create Your Quarterly Goals

What do you want to <u>accomplish?</u>

Before you embark on your journalling practice, put some thought into some goals that you'd like to accomplish. This journal is space enough for ninety days of journalling, so consider these goals your "Quarterly" goals. What do you want to accomplish in the next three months?

Putting your goals on paper is the first step to achieving them. Once you see what they are, it'll be easier to make decisions and actions that are well-suited to your intensions. <u>Then, dog-ear this page, and look at it every day before you start journalling.</u>

Choose goals in any area of your life that you like, but make them specific and timely so you know exactly *what* you want to do, and when you want to do it by.

Goal #1:

Goal #2:

Goal #3:

"On the difficult days,
when the world's on your shoulders,
remember that diamonds are made
under the weight of mountains."
-Beau Taplin

Date: _____

SELF-LOVE
#MomfidentAF
JOURNAL

Today I am grateful for:

Today I aim to accomplish:

1.

2.

3.

Movement plan for the day:

Something I love about my body/physical traits **RIGHT NOW**:

Something I love about my character/personality **RIGHT NOW**:

Today's affirmation(s):

(I CHOOSE TO... I AM... I WILL... I ACCEPT... I OBSERVE... I EMBRACE...)

Tone Setter :

"You yourself, as much as anybody in the entire
universe, deserve your love and affection."
-Buddha

SELF-LOVE
#MomfidentAF
JOURNAL

Date: _____

Today I am grateful for:

Today I aim to accomplish:

1.

2.

3.

Movement plan for the day:

Something I love about my body/physical traits <u>RIGHT NOW</u>:

Something I love about my character/personality <u>RIGHT NOW</u>:

Today's affirmation(s):

(I CHOOSE TO... I AM... I WILL... I ACCEPT... I OBSERVE... I EMBRACE...)

Tone Setter :

"Love yourself first and everything else falls into line.
You really have to love yourself to get anything done in the world."
-Lucille Ball

Date: _____

SELF-LOVE
#MomfidentAF
JOURNAL

Today I am grateful for:

Today I aim to accomplish:

1.

2.

3.

Movement plan for the day:

Something I love about my body/physical traits <u>RIGHT NOW</u>:

Something I love about my character/personality <u>RIGHT NOW</u>:

Today's affirmation(s):

(I CHOOSE TO... I AM... I WILL... I ACCEPT... I OBSERVE... I EMBRACE...)

Tone Setter :

"Remember that you not only have the right to be an individual,
you have an obligation to be one."
-Eleanor Roosevelt

Date: _____

SELF-LOVE
#MomfidentAF
JOURNAL

Today I am grateful for:

Today I aim to accomplish:

1.

2.

3.

Movement plan for the day:

Something I love about my body/physical traits <u>RIGHT NOW</u>:

Something I love about my character/personality <u>RIGHT NOW</u>:

Today's affirmation(s):

(I CHOOSE TO... I AM... I WILL... I ACCEPT... I OBSERVE... I EMBRACE...)

Tone Setter:

"Too many people overvalue what they are not
and undervalue what they are."
-Malcolm S. Forbes

SELF-LOVE
#MomfidentAF
JOURNAL

Date: _____

Today I am grateful for:

Today I aim to accomplish:

1.

2.

3.

Movement plan for the day:

Something I love about my body/physical traits <u>RIGHT NOW</u>:

Something I love about my character/personality <u>RIGHT NOW</u>:

Today's affirmation(s):

(I CHOOSE TO... I AM... I WILL... I ACCEPT... I OBSERVE... I EMBRACE...)

Tone Setter :

"Every time you complain,
you give up your opportunity to experience joy."
-Cara Alwill Leyba

Date: _____

SELF-LOVE
#MomfidentAF
JOURNAL

Today I am grateful for:

Today I aim to accomplish:

1.

2.

3.

Movement plan for the day:

Something I love about my body/physical traits <u>RIGHT NOW</u>:

Something I love about my character/personality <u>RIGHT NOW</u>:

Today's affirmation(s):

(I CHOOSE TO... I AM... I WILL... I ACCEPT... I OBSERVE... I EMBRACE...)

Tone Setter:

"Accept who you are, completely; the good and the bad,
and make changes as YOU see fit,
not because you think someone else wants you to be different."
-Stacey Charter

Date: _____

SELF-LOVE
#MomfidentAF
JOURNAL

Today I am grateful for:

Today I aim to accomplish:

1.

2.

3.

Movement plan for the day:

Something I love about my body/physical traits <u>RIGHT NOW</u>:

Something I love about my character/personality <u>RIGHT NOW</u>:

Today's affirmation(s):

(I CHOOSE TO... I AM... I WILL... I ACCEPT... I OBSERVE... I EMBRACE...)

Tone Setter :

"We ask ourselves, 'Who am I to be brilliant, gorgeous, talented, fabulous?' Actually, who are you not to be?"
-Marianne Williamson

Date: _____

SELF-LOVE
#MomfidentAF
JOURNAL

Today I am grateful for:

Today I aim to accomplish:

1.

2.

3.

Movement plan for the day:

Something I love about my body/physical traits <u>RIGHT NOW</u>:

Something I love about my character/personality <u>RIGHT NOW</u>:

Today's affirmation(s):

(I CHOOSE TO... I AM... I WILL... I ACCEPT... I OBSERVE... I EMBRACE...)

Tone Setter:

"We are what our thoughts have made us;
so take care about what you think.
Words are secondary. Thoughts live; they travel far."
-Swami Vivekananda

Date: _____

SELF-LOVE
#MomfidentAF
JOURNAL

Today I am grateful for:

Today I aim to accomplish:

1.

2.

3.

Movement plan for the day:

Something I love about my body/physical traits <u>RIGHT NOW</u>:

Something I love about my character/personality <u>RIGHT NOW</u>:

Today's affirmation(s):

(I CHOOSE TO... I AM... I WILL... I ACCEPT... I OBSERVE... I EMBRACE...)

Tone Setter :

"Be everything to you, not everything to everybody."
-Lisa Lieberman-Wang

Date: _____

SELF-LOVE
#MomfidentAF
JOURNAL

Today I am grateful for:

Today I aim to accomplish:

1.

2.

3.

Movement plan for the day:

Something I love about my body/physical traits <u>RIGHT NOW</u>:

Something I love about my character/personality <u>RIGHT NOW</u>:

Today's affirmation(s):

(I CHOOSE TO... I AM... I WILL... I ACCEPT... I OBSERVE... I EMBRACE...)

Tone Setter:

"You have been criticizing yourself for years, and it hasn't worked.
Try approving of yourself and see what happens."
-Louise L. Hay

Date: _____

SELF-LOVE
#MomfidentAF
JOURNAL

Today I am grateful for:

Today I aim to accomplish:

1.

2.

3.

Movement plan for the day:

Something I love about my body/physical traits <u>RIGHT NOW</u>:

Something I love about my character/personality <u>RIGHT NOW</u>:

Today's affirmation(s):

(I CHOOSE TO... I AM... I WILL... I ACCEPT... I OBSERVE... I EMBRACE...)

Tone Setter:

"Act as if what you do makes a difference. It does."
-William James

Date: _____

SELF-LOVE
#MomfidentAF
JOURNAL

Today I am grateful for:

Today I aim to accomplish:

1.

2.

3.

Movement plan for the day:

Something I love about my body/physical traits <u>RIGHT NOW</u>:

Something I love about my character/personality <u>RIGHT NOW</u>:

Today's affirmation(s):

{I CHOOSE TO... I AM... I WILL... I ACCEPT... I OBSERVE... I EMBRACE...}

Tone Setter :

"Because one believes in oneself, one doesn't try to convince others.
Because one is content with oneself, one doesn't need others' approval."
-Lao-Tzu

Date: _____

SELF-LOVE
#MomfidentAF
JOURNAL

Today I am grateful for:

Today I aim to accomplish:

1.

2.

3.

Movement plan for the day:

Something I love about my body/physical traits <u>RIGHT NOW</u>:

Something I love about my character/personality <u>RIGHT NOW</u>:

Today's affirmation(s):

{I CHOOSE TO... I AM... I WILL... I ACCEPT... I OBSERVE... I EMBRACE...}

Tone Setter:

"People who want the most approval get the least,
and the people who need approval the least get the most."
-Wayne Dyer

Date: _____

SELF-LOVE
#MomfidentAF
JOURNAL

Today I am grateful for:

Today I aim to accomplish:

1.

2.

3.

Movement plan for the day:

Something I love about my body/physical traits <u>RIGHT NOW</u>:

Something I love about my character/personality <u>RIGHT NOW</u>:

Today's affirmation(s):

(I CHOOSE TO... I AM... I WILL... I ACCEPT... I OBSERVE... I EMBRACE...)

Tone Setter:

"There is nothing noble about being superior to some other [person].
The true nobility is in being superior to your previous self."
-Hindu Proverb

Date: _____

SELF-LOVE
#MomfidentAF
JOURNAL

Today I am grateful for:

Today I aim to accomplish:

1.

2.

3.

Movement plan for the day:

Something I love about my body/physical traits <u>RIGHT NOW</u>:

Something I love about my character/personality <u>RIGHT NOW</u>:

Today's affirmation(s):

(I CHOOSE TO... I AM... I WILL... I ACCEPT... I OBSERVE... I EMBRACE...)

Tone Setter:

"If you aren't good at loving yourself,
you will have a difficult time loving anyone, since you'll resent the time
and energy you give another person that you aren't giving to yourself."
-Barbara De Angelis

Date: _____

SELF-LOVE
#MomfidentAF
JOURNAL

Today I am grateful for:

Today I aim to accomplish:

1.

2.

3.

Movement plan for the day:

Something I love about my body/physical traits <u>RIGHT NOW</u>:

Something I love about my character/personality <u>RIGHT NOW</u>:

Today's affirmation(s):

(I CHOOSE TO... I AM... I WILL... I ACCEPT... I OBSERVE... I EMBRACE...)

Tone Setter :

"There came a time when the risk to remain tight in a bud
was more painful than the risk it took to blossom."
-Anaïs Nin

Date: _____

SELF-LOVE
#MomfidentAF
JOURNAL

Today I am grateful for:

Today I aim to accomplish:

1.

2.

3.

Movement plan for the day:

Something I love about my body/physical traits <u>RIGHT NOW</u>:

Something I love about my character/personality <u>RIGHT NOW</u>:

Today's affirmation(s):

(I CHOOSE TO… I AM… I WILL… I ACCEPT… I OBSERVE… I EMBRACE…)

Tone Setter:

"When I loved myself enough, I began leaving whatever wasn't healthy.
This meant people, jobs, my own beliefs and habits
- anything that kept me small."
-Kim McMillen

Date: _____

SELF-LOVE
#MomfidentAF
JOURNAL

Today I am grateful for:

Today I aim to accomplish:

1.

2.

3.

Movement plan for the day:

Something I love about my body/physical traits <u>RIGHT NOW</u>:

Something I love about my character/personality <u>RIGHT NOW</u>:

Today's affirmation(s):

[I CHOOSE TO... I AM... I WILL... I ACCEPT... I OBSERVE... I EMBRACE...]

Tone Setter:

"Life is ten percent what you experience
and ninety percent how you respond to it."
-Dorothy M. Neddermeyer

Date: _____

SELF-LOVE
#MomfidentAF
JOURNAL

Today I am grateful for:

Today I aim to accomplish:

1.

2.

3.

Movement plan for the day:

Something I love about my body/physical traits <u>RIGHT NOW</u>:

Something I love about my character/personality <u>RIGHT NOW</u>:

Today's affirmation(s):

(I CHOOSE TO... I AM... I WILL... I ACCEPT... I OBSERVE... I EMBRACE...)

Tone Setter :

"To love yourself right now, just as you are, is to give yourself heaven.
Don't wait until you die. If you wait, you die now. If you love, you live now."
-Alan Cohen

Date: _____

SELF-LOVE
#MomfidentAF
JOURNAL

Today I am grateful for:

Today I aim to accomplish:

1.

2.

3.

Movement plan for the day:

Something I love about my body/physical traits <u>RIGHT NOW</u>:

Something I love about my character/personality <u>RIGHT NOW</u>:

Today's affirmation(s):

I CHOOSE TO... I AM... I WILL... I ACCEPT... I OBSERVE... I EMBRACE...

Tone Setter :

"Your playing small does not serve the world.
There is nothing enlightened about shrinking so that other people
won't feel insecure around you."
-Marianne Williamson

Date: _____

SELF-LOVE
#MomfidentAF
JOURNAL

Today I am grateful for:

Today I aim to accomplish:

1.

2.

3.

Movement plan for the day:

Something I love about my body/physical traits <u>RIGHT NOW</u>:

Something I love about my character/personality <u>RIGHT NOW</u>:

Today's affirmation(s):

{I CHOOSE TO... I AM... I WILL... I ACCEPT... I OBSERVE... I EMBRACE...}

Tone Setter :

"Owning our story and loving ourselves through that process
is the bravest thing that we'll ever do."
-Brené Brown

Date: _____

SELF-LOVE
#MomfidentAF
JOURNAL

Today I am grateful for:

Today I aim to accomplish:

1.

2.

3.

Movement plan for the day:

Something I love about my body/physical traits <u>RIGHT NOW</u>:

Something I love about my character/personality <u>RIGHT NOW</u>:

Today's affirmation(s):

{I CHOOSE TO... I AM... I WILL... I ACCEPT... I OBSERVE... I EMBRACE...}

Tone Setter :

"Above all, be true to yourself, and if you cannot put your heart in it,
take yourself out of it."
-Unknown

Date: _____

SELF-LOVE
#MomfidentAF
JOURNAL

Today I am grateful for:

Today I aim to accomplish:

1.

2.

3.

Movement plan for the day:

Something I love about my body/physical traits <u>RIGHT NOW</u>:

Something I love about my character/personality <u>RIGHT NOW</u>:

Today's affirmation(s):

(I CHOOSE TO... I AM... I WILL... I ACCEPT... I OBSERVE... I EMBRACE...)

Tone Setter :

"You have to believe in yourself when no one else does
- that makes you a winner right there."
-Venus Williams

Date: _____

SELF-LOVE
#MomfidentAF
JOURNAL

Today I am grateful for:

Today I aim to accomplish:

1.

2.

3.

Movement plan for the day:

Something I love about my body/physical traits <u>RIGHT NOW</u>:

Something I love about my character/personality <u>RIGHT NOW</u>:

Today's affirmation(s):

I CHOOSE TO... I AM... I WILL... I ACCEPT... I OBSERVE... I EMBRACE...

Tone Setter :

"The real difficulty is to overcome how you think about yourself."
-Maya Angelou

Date: _____

SELF-LOVE
#MomfidentAF
JOURNAL

Today I am grateful for:

Today I aim to accomplish:

1.

2.

3.

Movement plan for the day:

Something I love about my body/physical traits <u>RIGHT NOW</u>:

Something I love about my character/personality <u>RIGHT NOW</u>:

Today's affirmation(s):

(I CHOOSE TO... I AM... I WILL... I ACCEPT... I OBSERVE... I EMBRACE...)

Tone Setter:

"No one can make you feel inferior without your consent."
-Eleanor Roosevelt

SELF-LOVE
#MomfidentAF
JOURNAL

Date: _____

Today I am grateful for:

Today I aim to accomplish:

1.

2.

3.

Movement plan for the day:

Something I love about my body/physical traits __RIGHT NOW__:

Something I love about my character/personality __RIGHT NOW__:

Today's affirmation(s):

(I CHOOSE TO... I AM... I WILL... I ACCEPT... I OBSERVE... I EMBRACE...)

Tone Setter:

"In order to love who you are,
you cannot hate the experiences that shaped you."
-Andrea Dykstra

SELF-LOVE
#MomfidentAF
JOURNAL

Date: _____

Today I am grateful for:

Today I aim to accomplish:

1.

2.

3.

Movement plan for the day:

Something I love about my body/physical traits <u>RIGHT NOW</u>:

Something I love about my character/personality <u>RIGHT NOW</u>:

Today's affirmation(s):

(I CHOOSE TO... I AM... I WILL... I ACCEPT... I OBSERVE... I EMBRACE...)

Tone Setter :

"Remind yourself that you cannot fail at being yourself."
-Wayne Dyer

Date: _____

SELF-LOVE
#MomfidentAF
JOURNAL

Today I am grateful for:

Today I aim to accomplish:

1.

2.

3.

Movement plan for the day:

Something I love about my body/physical traits <u>RIGHT NOW</u>:

Something I love about my character/personality <u>RIGHT NOW</u>:

Today's affirmation(s):

[I CHOOSE TO... I AM... I WILL... I ACCEPT... I OBSERVE... I EMBRACE...]

Tone Setter:

"There is no sense in punishing your future for the mistakes of your past.
Forgive yourself, grow from it, and then let it go."
-Melanie Koulouris

Date: _____

SELF-LOVE
#MomfidentAF
JOURNAL

Today I am grateful for:

Today I aim to accomplish:

1.

2.

3.

Movement plan for the day:

Something I love about my body/physical traits <u>RIGHT NOW</u>:

Something I love about my character/personality <u>RIGHT NOW</u>:

Today's affirmation(s):

[I CHOOSE TO... I AM... I WILL... I ACCEPT... I OBSERVE... I EMBRACE...]

Tone Setter :

"Beauty begins the moment you decide to be yourself."
-Coco Chanel

Date: _____

SELF-LOVE
#MomfidentAF
JOURNAL

Today I am grateful for:

Today I aim to accomplish:

1.

2.

3.

Movement plan for the day:

Something I love about my body/physical traits <u>RIGHT NOW</u>:

Something I love about my character/personality <u>RIGHT NOW</u>:

Today's affirmation(s):

(I CHOOSE TO... I AM... I WILL... I ACCEPT... I OBSERVE... I EMBRACE...)

Tone Setter:

"To me, beauty is about being comfortable in your own skin.
It's about knowing and accepting who you are."
-Ellen Degeneres

Date: _____

SELF-LOVE
#MomfidentAF
JOURNAL

Today I am grateful for:

Today I aim to accomplish:

1.

2.

3.

Movement plan for the day:

Something I love about my body/physical traits <u>RIGHT NOW</u>:

Something I love about my character/personality <u>RIGHT NOW</u>:

Today's affirmation(s):

{I CHOOSE TO... I AM... I WILL... I ACCEPT... I OBSERVE... I EMBRACE...}

Tone Setter:

"You are no less valuable as a size 16 than a size 4.
You are no less valuable as a 32a than a 36c."
-Mary Lambert

Date: _____

SELF-LOVE
#MomfidentAF
JOURNAL

Today I am grateful for:

Today I aim to accomplish:

1.

2.

3.

Movement plan for the day:

Something I love about my body/physical traits <u>RIGHT NOW</u>:

Something I love about my character/personality <u>RIGHT NOW</u>:

Today's affirmation(s):

[I CHOOSE TO... I AM... I WILL... I ACCEPT... I OBSERVE... I EMBRACE...]

Tone Setter:

"[Confidence] doesn't have anything to do with
how the world perceives you. What matters is what you see."
-Gabourey Sidibe

Date: _____

SELF-LOVE
#MomfidentAF
JOURNAL

Today I am grateful for:

Today I aim to accomplish:

1.

2.

3.

Movement plan for the day:

Something I love about my body/physical traits <u>RIGHT NOW</u>:

Something I love about my character/personality <u>RIGHT NOW</u>:

Today's affirmation(s):

{I CHOOSE TO... I AM... I WILL... I ACCEPT... I OBSERVE... I EMBRACE...}

Tone Setter:

"You are imperfect, permanently and inevitably flawed.
And you are beautiful."
-Amy Bloom

Date: _____

SELF-LOVE
#MomfidentAF
JOURNAL

Today I am grateful for:

Today I aim to accomplish:

1.

2.

3.

Movement plan for the day:

Something I love about my body/physical traits <u>RIGHT NOW</u>:

Something I love about my character/personality <u>RIGHT NOW</u>:

Today's affirmation(s):

[I CHOOSE TO... I AM... I WILL... I ACCEPT... I OBSERVE... I EMBRACE...]

Tone Setter:

"By choosing healthy over skinny you are choosing self-love over self-judgement. You are beautiful."
-Steve Maraboli

Date: _____

SELF-LOVE
#MomfidentAF
JOURNAL

Today I am grateful for:

Today I aim to accomplish:

1.

2.

3.

Movement plan for the day:

Something I love about my body/physical traits <u>RIGHT NOW</u>:

Something I love about my character/personality <u>RIGHT NOW</u>:

Today's affirmation(s):

(I CHOOSE TO... I AM... I WILL... I ACCEPT... I OBSERVE... I EMBRACE...)

Tone Setter:

"The world will see you the way you see you,
and treat you the way you treat yourself."
-Beyoncé

Date: _____

SELF-LOVE
#MomfidentAF
JOURNAL

Today I am grateful for:

Today I aim to accomplish:

1.

2.

3.

Movement plan for the day:

Something I love about my body/physical traits <u>RIGHT NOW</u>:

Something I love about my character/personality <u>RIGHT NOW</u>:

Today's affirmation(s):

[I CHOOSE TO... I AM... I WILL... I ACCEPT... I OBSERVE... I EMBRACE...]

Tone Setter:

"The pursuit of excellence is gratifying and healthy.
The pursuit of perfection is frustrating and neurotic."
-Edwin Bliss

Date: _____

SELF-LOVE
#MomfidentAF
JOURNAL

Today I am grateful for:

Today I aim to accomplish:

1.

2.

3.

Movement plan for the day:

Something I love about my body/physical traits <u>RIGHT NOW</u>:

Something I love about my character/personality <u>RIGHT NOW</u>:

Today's affirmation(s):

(I CHOOSE TO... I AM... I WILL... I ACCEPT... I OBSERVE... I EMBRACE...)

Tone Setter:

"Never give up on a dream because of the time
it will take to accomplish it. The time will pass anyway."
-Earl Nightingale

Date: _____

SELF-LOVE
#MomfidentAF
JOURNAL

Today I am grateful for:

Today I aim to accomplish:

1.

2.

3.

Movement plan for the day:

Something I love about my body/physical traits <u>RIGHT NOW</u>:

Something I love about my character/personality <u>RIGHT NOW</u>:

Today's affirmation(s):

(I CHOOSE TO... I AM... I WILL... I ACCEPT... I OBSERVE... I EMBRACE...)

Tone Setter :

"Gratitude is the practice of shifting the focus from what's missing to what already exists."
-Cara Alwill Leyba

SELF-LOVE
#MomfidentAF
JOURNAL

Date: _____

Today I am grateful for:

Today I aim to accomplish:

1.

2.

3.

Movement plan for the day:

Something I love about my body/physical traits <u>RIGHT NOW</u>:

Something I love about my character/personality <u>RIGHT NOW</u>:

Today's affirmation(s):

{I CHOOSE TO... I AM... I WILL... I ACCEPT... I OBSERVE... I EMBRACE...}

Tone Setter:

"I am a strong woman with or without this person,
with or without this job, and with or without these tight pants."
-Queen Latifah

Date: _____

SELF-LOVE
#MomfidentAF
JOURNAL

Today I am grateful for:

Today I aim to accomplish:

1.

2.

3.

Movement plan for the day:

Something I love about my body/physical traits <u>RIGHT NOW</u>:

Something I love about my character/personality <u>RIGHT NOW</u>:

Today's affirmation(s):

(I CHOOSE TO... I AM... I WILL... I ACCEPT... I OBSERVE... I EMBRACE...)

Tone Setter :

"Once you awaken, you will have no interest
in judging those who sleep."
-James Blanchard

SELF-LOVE
#MomfidentAF
JOURNAL

Date: _____

Today I am grateful for:

Today I aim to accomplish:

1.

2.

3.

Movement plan for the day:

Something I love about my body/physical traits <u>RIGHT NOW</u>:

Something I love about my character/personality <u>RIGHT NOW</u>:

Today's affirmation(s):

(I CHOOSE TO... I AM... I WILL... I ACCEPT... I OBSERVE... I EMBRACE...)

Tone Setter:

"Being our messy, imperfect, authentic selves helps create a space
where others feel safe to be themselves, too."
-B. Oakman

Date: _____

SELF-LOVE
#MomfidentAF
JOURNAL

Today I am grateful for:

Today I aim to accomplish:

1.

2.

3.

Movement plan for the day:

Something I love about my body/physical traits <u>RIGHT NOW</u>:

Something I love about my character/personality <u>RIGHT NOW</u>:

Today's affirmation(s):

(I CHOOSE TO... I AM... I WILL... I ACCEPT... I OBSERVE... I EMBRACE...)

Tone Setter:

"A river cuts through rock not by power, but by persistence."
-Jim Watkins

SELF-LOVE
#MomfidentAF
JOURNAL

Date: _____

Today I am grateful for:

Today I aim to accomplish:

1.

2.

3.

Movement plan for the day:

Something I love about my body/physical traits <u>RIGHT NOW</u>:

Something I love about my character/personality <u>RIGHT NOW</u>:

Today's affirmation(s):

{I CHOOSE TO... I AM... I WILL... I ACCEPT... I OBSERVE... I EMBRACE...}

Tone Setter :

"Absorb what is useful, discard what is not,
add what is uniquely your own."
-Bruce Lee

Date: _____

SELF-LOVE
#MomfidentAF
JOURNAL

Today I am grateful for:

Today I aim to accomplish:

1.

2.

3.

Movement plan for the day:

Something I love about my body/physical traits <u>RIGHT NOW</u>:

Something I love about my character/personality <u>RIGHT NOW</u>:

Today's affirmation(s):

I CHOOSE TO... I AM... I WILL... I ACCEPT... I OBSERVE... I EMBRACE...

Tone Setter:

"If you compare yourself to others, you may become vain and bitter;
for there are always greater and lesser persons than yourself."
-Desiderata

Date: _____

SELF-LOVE
#MomfidentAF
JOURNAL

Today I am grateful for:

Today I aim to accomplish:

1.

2.

3.

Movement plan for the day:

Something I love about my body/physical traits <u>RIGHT NOW</u>:

Something I love about my character/personality <u>RIGHT NOW</u>:

Today's affirmation(s):

(I CHOOSE TO... I AM... I WILL... I ACCEPT... I OBSERVE... I EMBRACE...)

Tone Setter:

"Stop trying to be less of who you are. Let this time in your life cut you open and drain all of the things that are holding you back."
-Jennifer Elisabeth

Date: _____

SELF-LOVE
#MomfidentAF
JOURNAL

Today I am grateful for:

Today I aim to accomplish:

1.

2.

3.

Movement plan for the day:

Something I love about my body/physical traits <u>RIGHT NOW</u>:

Something I love about my character/personality <u>RIGHT NOW</u>:

Today's affirmation(s):

I CHOOSE TO... I AM... I WILL... I ACCEPT... I OBSERVE... I EMBRACE...

Tone Setter:

"You find peace not by rearranging the circumstances of your life,
but by realizing who you are at the deepest level."
-Eckhart Tolle

Date: _____

SELF-LOVE
#MomfidentAF
JOURNAL

Today I am grateful for:

Today I aim to accomplish:

1.

2.

3.

Movement plan for the day:

Something I love about my body/physical traits <u>RIGHT NOW</u>:

Something I love about my character/personality <u>RIGHT NOW</u>:

Today's affirmation(s):

(I CHOOSE TO... I AM... I WILL... I ACCEPT... I OBSERVE... I EMBRACE...)

Tone Setter :

"When a woman becomes her own best friend, life is easier."
-Diane Von Furstenberg

Date: _____

SELF-LOVE
#MomfidentAF
JOURNAL

Today I am grateful for:

Today I aim to accomplish:

1.

2.

3.

Movement plan for the day:

Something I love about my body/physical traits <u>RIGHT NOW</u>:

Something I love about my character/personality <u>RIGHT NOW</u>:

Today's affirmation(s):

(I CHOOSE TO... I AM... I WILL... I ACCEPT... I OBSERVE... I EMBRACE...)

Tone Setter:

"Document the moments you feel most in love with yourself
- what you're wearing, who you're around, what you're doing.
Recreate and repeat."
-Warsan Shire

Date: _____

SELF-LOVE
#MomfidentAF
JOURNAL

Today I am grateful for:

Today I aim to accomplish:

1.

2.

3.

Movement plan for the day:

Something I love about my body/physical traits <u>RIGHT NOW</u>:

Something I love about my character/personality <u>RIGHT NOW</u>:

Today's affirmation(s):

(I CHOOSE TO... I AM... I WILL... I ACCEPT... I OBSERVE... I EMBRACE...)

Tone Setter:

"One of the greatest regrets in life is being
what others would want you to be, rather than being yourself."
-Shannon L. Alder

Date: _____

SELF-LOVE
#MomfidentAF
JOURNAL

Today I am grateful for:

Today I aim to accomplish:

1.

2.

3.

Movement plan for the day:

Something I love about my body/physical traits <u>RIGHT NOW</u>:

Something I love about my character/personality <u>RIGHT NOW</u>:

Today's affirmation(s):

I CHOOSE TO... I AM... I WILL... I ACCEPT... I OBSERVE... I EMBRACE...

Tone Setter :

"The bravest thing you can do is stop caring so much about
what other people think about you."
-Courtney St Croix

SELF-LOVE
#MomfidentAF
JOURNAL

Date: _____

Today I am grateful for:

Today I aim to accomplish:

1.

2.

3.

Movement plan for the day:

Something I love about my body/physical traits <u>RIGHT NOW</u>:

Something I love about my character/personality <u>RIGHT NOW</u>:

Today's affirmation(s):

(I CHOOSE TO... I AM... I WILL... I ACCEPT... I OBSERVE... I EMBRACE...)

Tone Setter:

"...sometimes you don't see the millions of people who accept you
for what you are. All you notice is the person who doesn't."
-Jodi Picoult

SELF-LOVE
#MomfidentAF
JOURNAL

Date: _____

Today I am grateful for:

Today I aim to accomplish:

1.

2.

3.

Movement plan for the day:

Something I love about my body/physical traits <u>RIGHT NOW</u>:

Something I love about my character/personality <u>RIGHT NOW</u>:

Today's affirmation(s):

(I CHOOSE TO... I AM... I WILL... I ACCEPT... I OBSERVE... I EMBRACE...)

Tone Setter:

"Your past is gone. Your mistakes are behind you.
Focus on your gorgeous, love-filled future."
-Cara Alwill Leyba

SELF-LOVE
#MomfidentAF
JOURNAL

Date: _____

Today I am grateful for:

Today I aim to accomplish:

1.

2.

3.

Movement plan for the day:

Something I love about my body/physical traits **RIGHT NOW**:

Something I love about my character/personality **RIGHT NOW**:

Today's affirmation(s):

(I CHOOSE TO... I AM... I WILL... I ACCEPT... I OBSERVE... I EMBRACE...)

Tone Setter :

"Love yourself enough to set boundaries.
Your time and energy are precious. You get to choose how you use it."
-Anna Taylor

Date: _____

SELF-LOVE
#MomfidentAF
JOURNAL

Today I am grateful for:

Today I aim to accomplish:

1.

2.

3.

Movement plan for the day:

Something I love about my body/physical traits <u>RIGHT NOW</u>:

Something I love about my character/personality <u>RIGHT NOW</u>:

Today's affirmation(s):

(I CHOOSE TO... I AM... I WILL... I ACCEPT... I OBSERVE... I EMBRACE...)

Tone Setter:

"The fact that someone else loves you doesn't rescue you from
the project of loving yourself."
-Sahaj Kohli

SELF-LOVE
#MomfidentAF
JOURNAL

Date: _____

Today I am grateful for:

Today I aim to accomplish:

1.

2.

3.

Movement plan for the day:

Something I love about my body/physical traits <u>RIGHT NOW</u>:

Something I love about my character/personality <u>RIGHT NOW</u>:

Today's affirmation(s):

(I CHOOSE TO... I AM... I WILL... I ACCEPT... I OBSERVE... I EMBRACE...)

Tone Setter:

"The most alluring thing a woman can have is confidence."
-Beyoncé

Date: _____

SELF-LOVE
#MomfidentAF
JOURNAL

Today I am grateful for:

Today I aim to accomplish:

1.

2.

3.

Movement plan for the day:

Something I love about my body/physical traits <u>RIGHT NOW</u>:

Something I love about my character/personality <u>RIGHT NOW</u>:

Today's affirmation(s):

(I CHOOSE TO... I AM... I WILL... I ACCEPT... I OBSERVE... I EMBRACE...)

Tone Setter:

"Look for a way to lift someone up.
And if that's all you do, that's enough."
-Elizabeth Lesser

SELF-LOVE
#MomfidentAF
JOURNAL

Date: _____

Today I am grateful for:

Today I aim to accomplish:

1.

2.

3.

Movement plan for the day:

Something I love about my body/physical traits <u>RIGHT NOW</u>:

Something I love about my character/personality <u>RIGHT NOW</u>:

Today's affirmation(s):

{I CHOOSE TO... I AM... I WILL... I ACCEPT... I OBSERVE... I EMBRACE...}

Tone Setter:

"Success is liking yourself, liking what you do, and how you do it."
-Maya Angelou

Date: _____

SELF-LOVE
#MomfidentAF
JOURNAL

Today I am grateful for:

Today I aim to accomplish:

1.

2.

3.

Movement plan for the day:

Something I love about my body/physical traits <u>RIGHT NOW</u>:

Something I love about my character/personality <u>RIGHT NOW</u>:

Today's affirmation(s):

(I CHOOSE TO... I AM... I WILL... I ACCEPT... I OBSERVE... I EMBRACE...)

Tone Setter:

"You need to learn how to select your thoughts just the same way
you select your clothes every day."
-Elizabeth Gilbert

Date: _____

SELF-LOVE
#MomfidentAF
JOURNAL

Today I am grateful for:

Today I aim to accomplish:

1.

2.

3.

Movement plan for the day:

Something I love about my body/physical traits <u>RIGHT NOW</u>:

Something I love about my character/personality <u>RIGHT NOW</u>:

Today's affirmation(s):

{I CHOOSE TO... I AM... I WILL... I ACCEPT... I OBSERVE... I EMBRACE...}

Tone Setter :

"All we have is all we need. All we need is the awareness
of how blessed we really are."
-Sarah Ban Breathnach

Date: _____

SELF-LOVE
#MomfidentAF
JOURNAL

Today I am grateful for:

Today I aim to accomplish:

1.

2.

3.

Movement plan for the day:

Something I love about my body/physical traits <u>RIGHT NOW</u>:

Something I love about my character/personality <u>RIGHT NOW</u>:

Today's affirmation(s):

(I CHOOSE TO... I AM... I WILL... I ACCEPT... I OBSERVE... I EMBRACE...)

Tone Setter :

"Self love has very little to do with how you feel about your outer self.
It's about accepting all of yourself."
-Tyra Banks

Date: _____

Today I am grateful for:

Today I aim to accomplish:

1.

2.

3.

Movement plan for the day:

Something I love about my body/physical traits <u>RIGHT NOW</u>:

Something I love about my character/personality <u>RIGHT NOW</u>:

Today's affirmation(s):

{I CHOOSE TO... I AM... I WILL... I ACCEPT... I OBSERVE... I EMBRACE...}

Tone Setter:

"Deal with yourself as an individual worthy of respect,
and make everyone else deal with you in the same way."
-Nikki Giovanni

Date: _____

SELF-LOVE
#MomfidentAF
JOURNAL

Today I am grateful for:

Today I aim to accomplish:

1.

2.

3.

Movement plan for the day:

Something I love about my body/physical traits <u>RIGHT NOW</u>:

Something I love about my character/personality <u>RIGHT NOW</u>:

Today's affirmation(s):

{I CHOOSE TO... I AM... I WILL... I ACCEPT... I OBSERVE... I EMBRACE...}

Tone Setter:

"The reward for conformity is that everyone likes you but yourself."
-Rita Mae Brown

Date: _____

SELF-LOVE
#MomfidentAF
JOURNAL

Today I am grateful for:

Today I aim to accomplish:

1.

2.

3.

Movement plan for the day:

Something I love about my body/physical traits <u>RIGHT NOW</u>:

Something I love about my character/personality <u>RIGHT NOW</u>:

Today's affirmation(s):

(I CHOOSE TO… I AM… I WILL… I ACCEPT… I OBSERVE… I EMBRACE…)

Tone Setter :

"Trust yourself. Think for yourself. Act for yourself. Speak for yourself.
Be yourself. Imitation is suicide."
-Marva Collins

Date: _____

SELF-LOVE
#MomfidentAF
JOURNAL

Today I am grateful for:

Today I aim to accomplish:

1.

2.

3.

Movement plan for the day:

Something I love about my body/physical traits <u>RIGHT NOW</u>:

Something I love about my character/personality <u>RIGHT NOW</u>:

Today's affirmation(s):

[I CHOOSE TO... I AM... I WILL... I ACCEPT... I OBSERVE... I EMBRACE...]

Tone Setter :

"Be strong enough to stand alone, smart enough to know
when you need help, and brave enough to ask for it."
-Ziad K. Abedelnour

Date: _____

SELF-LOVE
#MomfidentAF
JOURNAL

Today I am grateful for:

Today I aim to accomplish:

1.

2.

3.

Movement plan for the day:

Something I love about my body/physical traits <u>RIGHT NOW</u>:

Something I love about my character/personality <u>RIGHT NOW</u>:

Today's affirmation(s):

(I CHOOSE TO... I AM... I WILL... I ACCEPT... I OBSERVE... I EMBRACE...)

Tone Setter:

"Don't rely on someone else for your happiness and self-worth.
Only you can be responsible for that. If you can't love and respect yourself,
no one else will be able to make that happen."
-Stacey Charter

Date: _____

SELF-LOVE
#MomfidentAF
JOURNAL

Today I am grateful for:

Today I aim to accomplish:

1.

2.

3.

Movement plan for the day:

Something I love about my body/physical traits <u>RIGHT NOW</u>:

Something I love about my character/personality <u>RIGHT NOW</u>:

Today's affirmation(s):

(I CHOOSE TO... I AM... I WILL... I ACCEPT... I OBSERVE... I EMBRACE...)

Tone Setter:

"Whatever is bringing you down, get rid of it.
Because you'll find that when you're free, your true self comes out."
-Tina Turner

SELF-LOVE
#MomfidentAF
JOURNAL

Date: _____

Today I am grateful for:

Today I aim to accomplish:

1.

2.

3.

Movement plan for the day:

Something I love about my body/physical traits <u>RIGHT NOW</u>:

Something I love about my character/personality <u>RIGHT NOW</u>:

Today's affirmation(s):

(I CHOOSE TO... I AM... I WILL... I ACCEPT... I OBSERVE... I EMBRACE...)

Tone Setter:

"The kind of beauty I want most is the hard-to-get
kind that comes from within - strength, courage, dignity."
-Ruby Dee

Date: _____

SELF-LOVE
#MomfidentAF
JOURNAL

Today I am grateful for:

Today I aim to accomplish:

1.

2.

3.

Movement plan for the day:

Something I love about my body/physical traits <u>RIGHT NOW</u>:

Something I love about my character/personality <u>RIGHT NOW</u>:

Today's affirmation(s):

(I CHOOSE TO... I AM... I WILL... I ACCEPT... I OBSERVE... I EMBRACE...)

Tone Setter :

"Whatever someone did to you in the past has no power over the present.
Only you give it power."
-Oprah Winfrey

SELF-LOVE
#MomfidentAF
JOURNAL

Date: _____

Today I am grateful for:

Today I aim to accomplish:

1.

2.

3.

Movement plan for the day:

Something I love about my body/physical traits <u>RIGHT NOW</u>:

Something I love about my character/personality <u>RIGHT NOW</u>:

Today's affirmation(s):

(I CHOOSE TO... I AM... I WILL... I ACCEPT... I OBSERVE... I EMBRACE...)

Tone Setter :

"Don't wait around for other people to be happy for you.
Any happiness you get you've got to make yourself."
-Alice Walker

Date: _____

SELF-LOVE
#MomfidentAF
JOURNAL

Today I am grateful for:

Today I aim to accomplish:

1.

2.

3.

Movement plan for the day:

Something I love about my body/physical traits <u>RIGHT NOW</u>:

Something I love about my character/personality <u>RIGHT NOW</u>:

Today's affirmation(s):

(I CHOOSE TO... I AM... I WILL... I ACCEPT... I OBSERVE... I EMBRACE...)

Tone Setter :

"Lighten up on yourself. No one is perfect.
Gently accept your humanness."
-Deborah Day

Date: _____

SELF-LOVE
#MomfidentAF
JOURNAL

Today I am grateful for:

Today I aim to accomplish:

1.

2.

3.

Movement plan for the day:

Something I love about my body/physical traits <u>RIGHT NOW</u>:

Something I love about my character/personality <u>RIGHT NOW</u>:

Today's affirmation(s):

(I CHOOSE TO... I AM... I WILL... I ACCEPT... I OBSERVE... I EMBRACE...)

Tone Setter :

"We have to reshape our own perception of how we view ourselves."
-Beyoncé

Date: _____

SELF-LOVE
#MomfidentAF
JOURNAL

Today I am grateful for:

Today I aim to accomplish:

1.

2.

3.

Movement plan for the day:

Something I love about my body/physical traits <u>RIGHT NOW</u>:

Something I love about my character/personality <u>RIGHT NOW</u>:

Today's affirmation(s):

{I CHOOSE TO... I AM... I WILL... I ACCEPT... I OBSERVE... I EMBRACE...}

Tone Setter:

"Growth begins when we start to accept our own weakness."
-Jean Vanier

Date: _____

SELF-LOVE
#MomfidentAF
JOURNAL

Today I am grateful for:

Today I aim to accomplish:

1.

2.

3.

Movement plan for the day:

Something I love about my body/physical traits <u>RIGHT NOW</u>:

Something I love about my character/personality <u>RIGHT NOW</u>:

Today's affirmation(s):

(I CHOOSE TO... I AM... I WILL... I ACCEPT... I OBSERVE... I EMBRACE...)

Tone Setter :

"Plant your own garden and decorate your own soul,
instead of waiting for someone to bring you flowers."
-Veronica A. Shoffstall

Date: _____

SELF-LOVE
#MomfidentAF
JOURNAL

Today I am grateful for:

Today I aim to accomplish:

1.

2.

3.

Movement plan for the day:

Something I love about my body/physical traits <u>RIGHT NOW</u>:

Something I love about my character/personality <u>RIGHT NOW</u>:

Today's affirmation(s):

(I CHOOSE TO... I AM... I WILL... I ACCEPT... I OBSERVE... I EMBRACE...)

Tone Setter :

"Whatever you are doing, love yourself for doing it.
Whatever you are feeling, love yourself for feeling it."
-Thaddeus Golas

Date: _____

SELF-LOVE
#MomfidentAF
JOURNAL

Today I am grateful for:

Today I aim to accomplish:

1.

2.

3.

Movement plan for the day:

Something I love about my body/physical traits <u>RIGHT NOW</u>:

Something I love about my character/personality <u>RIGHT NOW</u>:

Today's affirmation(s):

I CHOOSE TO... I AM... I WILL... I ACCEPT... I OBSERVE... I EMBRACE...

Tone Setter:

"Find the love you seek, by first finding the love within yourself.
Learn to rest in that place within you that is your true home."
-Sri Sri Ravi Shankar

Date: _____

SELF-LOVE
#MomfidentAF
JOURNAL

Today I am grateful for:

Today I aim to accomplish:

1.

2.

3.

Movement plan for the day:

Something I love about my body/physical traits <u>RIGHT NOW</u>:

Something I love about my character/personality <u>RIGHT NOW</u>:

Today's affirmation(s):

(I CHOOSE TO... I AM... I WILL... I ACCEPT... I OBSERVE... I EMBRACE...)

Tone Setter :

"Loving yourself does not mean self-absorbed or narcissistic,
or disregarding others. Rather it means welcoming yourself as the most honoured
guest in your own heart, a guest worthy of respect, a loveable companion."
-Margo Anand

Date: _____

SELF-LOVE
#MomfidentAF
JOURNAL

Today I am grateful for:

Today I aim to accomplish:

1.

2.

3.

Movement plan for the day:

Something I love about my body/physical traits <u>RIGHT NOW</u>:

Something I love about my character/personality <u>RIGHT NOW</u>:

Today's affirmation(s):

(I CHOOSE TO... I AM... I WILL... I ACCEPT... I OBSERVE... I EMBRACE...)

Tone Setter :

"Love is the great miracle cure.
Loving ourselves works miracles in our lives."
-Louise L. Hay

Date: _____

SELF-LOVE
#MomfidentAF
JOURNAL

Today I am grateful for:

Today I aim to accomplish:

1.

2.

3.

Movement plan for the day:

Something I love about my body/physical traits <u>RIGHT NOW</u>:

Something I love about my character/personality <u>RIGHT NOW</u>:

Today's affirmation(s):

(I CHOOSE TO... I AM... I WILL... I ACCEPT... I OBSERVE... I EMBRACE...)

Tone Setter :

"You can't build joy on a feeling of self-loathing."
-Ram Dass

Date: _____

SELF-LOVE
#MomfidentAF
JOURNAL

Today I am grateful for:

Today I aim to accomplish:

1.

2.

3.

Movement plan for the day:

Something I love about my body/physical traits <u>RIGHT NOW</u>:

Something I love about my character/personality <u>RIGHT NOW</u>:

Today's affirmation(s):

(I CHOOSE TO... I AM... I WILL... I ACCEPT... I OBSERVE... I EMBRACE...)

Tone Setter :

"Your task is not to seek for love, but merely to seek and find all
the barriers within yourself that you have built against it."
-Rumi

Date: _____

SELF-LOVE
#MomfidentAF
JOURNAL

Today I am grateful for:

Today I aim to accomplish:

1.

2.

3.

Movement plan for the day:

Something I love about my body/physical traits <u>RIGHT NOW</u>:

Something I love about my character/personality <u>RIGHT NOW</u>:

Today's affirmation(s):

[I CHOOSE TO... I AM... I WILL... I ACCEPT... I OBSERVE... I EMBRACE...]

Tone Setter:

"Believing in our hearts that who we are is enough is the key to
a more satisfying and balanced life."
-Ellen Sue Stern

Date: _____

SELF-LOVE
#MomfidentAF
JOURNAL

Today I am grateful for:

Today I aim to accomplish:

1.

2.

3.

Movement plan for the day:

Something I love about my body/physical traits <u>RIGHT NOW</u>:

Something I love about my character/personality <u>RIGHT NOW</u>:

Today's affirmation(s):

[I CHOOSE TO... I AM... I WILL... I ACCEPT... I OBSERVE... I EMBRACE...]

Tone Setter :

"To accept ourselves as we are means to value our imperfections
as much as our perfections."
-Sandra Bierig

Date: _____

SELF-LOVE
#MomfidentAF
JOURNAL

Today I am grateful for:

Today I aim to accomplish:

1.

2.

3.

Movement plan for the day:

Something I love about my body/physical traits <u>RIGHT NOW</u>:

Something I love about my character/personality <u>RIGHT NOW</u>:

Today's affirmation(s):

(I CHOOSE TO... I AM... I WILL... I ACCEPT... I OBSERVE... I EMBRACE...)

Tone Setter :

"The problem is you're ... too busy holding onto your unworthiness."
-Ram Dass

Date: _____

SELF-LOVE
#MomfidentAF
JOURNAL

Today I am grateful for:

Today I aim to accomplish:

1.

2.

3.

Movement plan for the day:

Something I love about my body/physical traits <u>RIGHT NOW</u>:

Something I love about my character/personality <u>RIGHT NOW</u>:

Today's affirmation(s):

(I CHOOSE TO... I AM... I WILL... I ACCEPT... I OBSERVE... I EMBRACE...)

Tone Setter:

"To be beautiful means to be yourself.
You don't need to be accepted by others. You need to accept yourself."
-Thich Nhat Hanh

Date: _____

SELF-LOVE
#MombidentAF
JOURNAL

Today I am grateful for:

Today I aim to accomplish:

1.

2.

3.

Movement plan for the day:

Something I love about my body/physical traits <u>RIGHT NOW</u>:

Something I love about my character/personality <u>RIGHT NOW</u>:

Today's affirmation(s):

(I CHOOSE TO... I AM... I WILL... I ACCEPT... I OBSERVE... I EMBRACE...)

Tone Setter:

"Scarcity of self value cannot be remedied by money,
recognition, affection, attention or influence."
-Gary Zukav

Date: _____

SELF-LOVE
#MomfidentAF
JOURNAL

Today I am grateful for:

Today I aim to accomplish:

1.

2.

3.

Movement plan for the day:

Something I love about my body/physical traits <u>RIGHT NOW</u>:

Something I love about my character/personality <u>RIGHT NOW</u>:

Today's affirmation(s):

(I CHOOSE TO… I AM… I WILL… I ACCEPT… I OBSERVE… I EMBRACE…)

Tone Setter :

"Too many people overvalue what they are not
and undervalue what they are."
-Malcolm S. Forbes

Date: _____

SELF-LOVE
#MomfidentAF
JOURNAL

Today I am grateful for:

Today I aim to accomplish:

1.

2.

3.

Movement plan for the day:

Something I love about my body/physical traits <u>RIGHT NOW</u>:

Something I love about my character/personality <u>RIGHT NOW</u>:

Today's affirmation(s):

{I CHOOSE TO... I AM... I WILL... I ACCEPT... I OBSERVE... I EMBRACE...}

Tone Setter :

"Most of the shadows of this life are caused
by standing in one's own sunshine."
-Ralph Waldo Emerson

Date: _____

Today I am grateful for:

Today I aim to accomplish:

1.

2.

3.

Movement plan for the day:

Something I love about my body/physical traits <u>RIGHT NOW</u>:

Something I love about my character/personality <u>RIGHT NOW</u>:

Today's affirmation(s):

[I CHOOSE TO... I AM... I WILL... I ACCEPT... I OBSERVE... I EMBRACE...]

Tone Setter :

"She lacks confidence, she craves admiration insatiably.
She lives on the reflections of herself in the eyes of others.
She does not dare to be herself."
-Anaïs Nin

Date: _____

SELF-LOVE
#MomfidentAF
JOURNAL

Today I am grateful for:

Today I aim to accomplish:

1.

2.

3.

Movement plan for the day:

Something I love about my body/physical traits <u>RIGHT NOW</u>:

Something I love about my character/personality <u>RIGHT NOW</u>:

Today's affirmation(s):

{I CHOOSE TO... I AM... I WILL... I ACCEPT... I OBSERVE... I EMBRACE...}

Tone Setter:

"The hardest challenge is to be yourself in a world
where everyone is trying to make you somebody else."
-E. E. Cummings

SELF-LOVE
#MomfidentAF
JOURNAL

Date: _____

Today I am grateful for:

Today I aim to accomplish:

1.

2.

3.

Movement plan for the day:

Something I love about my body/physical traits <u>RIGHT NOW</u>:

Something I love about my character/personality <u>RIGHT NOW</u>:

Today's affirmation(s):

(I CHOOSE TO… I AM… I WILL… I ACCEPT… I OBSERVE… I EMBRACE…)

Tone Setter :

"People are like stained-glass windows. They sparkle when the sun is out,
but when the darkness sets in, their true beauty is revealed
only if there is a light from within."
-Elisabeth Kübler-Ross

Date: _____

SELF-LOVE
#MomfidentAF
JOURNAL

Today I am grateful for:

Today I aim to accomplish:

1.

2.

3.

Movement plan for the day:

Something I love about my body/physical traits <u>RIGHT NOW</u>:

Something I love about my character/personality <u>RIGHT NOW</u>:

Today's affirmation(s):

{I CHOOSE TO... I AM... I WILL... I ACCEPT... I OBSERVE... I EMBRACE...}

Tone Setter:

"Becoming acquainted with yourself is a price well worth paying
for the love that will really address your needs."
-Daphne Rose Kingma

SELF-LOVE
#MomfidentAF
JOURNAL

Date: _____

Today I am grateful for:

Today I aim to accomplish:

1.

2.

3.

Movement plan for the day:

Something I love about my body/physical traits <u>RIGHT NOW</u>:

Something I love about my character/personality <u>RIGHT NOW</u>:

Today's affirmation(s):

I CHOOSE TO... I AM... I WILL... I ACCEPT... I OBSERVE... I EMBRACE...

Tone Setter :

"What lies behind us and what lies before us are tiny matters
compared to what lies within us."
-Ralph Waldo Emerson

Date: _____

SELF-LOVE
#1MomfidentAF
JOURNAL

Today I am grateful for:

Today I aim to accomplish:

1.

2.

3.

Movement plan for the day:

Something I love about my body/physical traits <u>RIGHT NOW</u>:

Something I love about my character/personality <u>RIGHT NOW</u>:

Today's affirmation(s):

(I CHOOSE TO... I AM... I WILL... I ACCEPT... I OBSERVE... I EMBRACE...)

Tone Setter:

"We are each gifted in a unique and important way.
It is our privilege and our adventure to discover our own special light."
-Mary Dunbar

Date: _____

SELF-LOVE
#MomfidentAF
JOURNAL

Today I am grateful for:

Today I aim to accomplish:

1.

2.

3.

Movement plan for the day:

Something I love about my body/physical traits <u>RIGHT NOW</u>:

Something I love about my character/personality <u>RIGHT NOW</u>:

Today's affirmation(s):

(I CHOOSE TO... I AM... I WILL... I ACCEPT... I OBSERVE... I EMBRACE...)

Tone Setter :

"Who looks outside, dreams;
who looks inside, awakes."
-Carl Jung

Notes n' Stuff:

Notes n' Stuff:

_____

_____

_____

_____

_____

_____

_____

_____

_____

_____

_____

_____

_____

_____

_____

_____

_____

_____

_____

Notes n' Stuff:

_____

_____

_____

_____

_____

_____

_____

_____

_____

_____

_____

_____

_____

_____

_____

_____

_____

_____

Notes n' Stuff:

Notes n' Stuff:

_____

_____

_____

_____

_____

_____

_____

_____

_____

_____

_____

_____

_____

_____

_____

_____

_____

_____

_____

_____

_____

_____

Notes n' Stuff:

_____

_____

_____

_____

_____

_____

_____

_____

_____

_____

_____

_____

_____

_____

_____

_____

_____

_____

_____

Notes n' Stuff:

Notes n' Stuff:

_____

_____

_____

_____

_____

_____

_____

_____

_____

_____

_____

_____

_____

_____

_____

_____

_____

_____

_____

_____

Notes n' Stuff:

_____

_____

_____

_____

_____

_____

_____

_____

_____

_____

_____

_____

_____

_____

_____

_____

_____

_____

_____

_____

Notes n' Stuff:

_____

_____

_____

_____

_____

_____

_____

_____

_____

_____

_____

_____

_____

_____

_____

_____

_____

_____

_____

Notes n' Stuff:

Notes n' Stuff:

_____

_____

_____

_____

_____

_____

_____

_____

_____

_____

_____

_____

_____

_____

_____

_____

_____

_____

_____

_____

Notes n' Stuff:

_____

_____

_____

_____

_____

_____

_____

_____

_____

_____

_____

_____

_____

_____

_____

_____

_____

_____

Notes n' Stuff:

Notes n' Stuff:

Notes n' Stuff:

_____

_____

_____

_____

_____

_____

_____

_____

_____

_____

_____

_____

_____

_____

_____

_____

_____

_____

_____

_____

_____

Notes n' Stuff:

Notes n' Stuff:

_____

_____

_____

_____

_____

_____

_____

_____

_____

_____

_____

_____

_____

_____

_____

_____

_____

_____

_____

_____

Notes n' Stuff:

Notes n' Stuff:

Notes n' Stuff:

_____

_____

_____

_____

_____

_____

_____

_____

_____

_____

_____

_____

_____

_____

_____

_____

_____

_____

Notes n' Stuff:

_____

_____

_____

_____

_____

_____

_____

_____

_____

_____

_____

_____

_____

_____

_____

_____

_____

_____

_____

_____

_____

Notes n' Stuff:

Notes n' Stuff:

_____

_____

_____

_____

_____

_____

_____

_____

_____

_____

_____

_____

_____

_____

_____

_____

_____

_____

_____

Notes n' Stuff:

Notes n' Stuff:

_____

_____

_____

_____

_____

_____

_____

_____

_____

_____

_____

_____

_____

_____

_____

_____

_____

_____

_____

_____

_____

Notes n' Stuff:

_____

_____

_____

_____

_____

_____

_____

_____

_____

_____

_____

_____

_____

_____

_____

_____

_____

_____

Notes n' Stuff:

Notes n' Stuff:

_____

_____

_____

_____

_____

_____

_____

_____

_____

_____

_____

_____

_____

_____

_____

_____

_____

_____

_____

_____

Notes n' Stuff:

_____

_____

_____

_____

_____

_____

_____

_____

_____

_____

_____

_____

_____

_____

_____

_____

_____

_____

_____

_____

_____

Notes n' Stuff:

_____

_____

_____

_____

_____

_____

_____

_____

_____

_____

_____

_____

_____

_____

_____

_____

_____

_____

_____

Notes n' Stuff:

_____

_____

_____

_____

_____

_____

_____

_____

_____

_____

_____

_____

_____

_____

_____

_____

_____

_____

_____

_____

Notes n' Stuff:

_____

_____

_____

_____

_____

_____

_____

_____

_____

_____

_____

_____

_____

_____

_____

_____

_____

_____

_____

Notes n' Stuff:

_____

_____

_____

_____

_____

_____

_____

_____

_____

_____

_____

_____

_____

_____

_____

_____

_____

_____

_____

_____

_____

Notes n' Stuff:

_____

_____

_____

_____

_____

_____

_____

_____

_____

_____

_____

_____

_____

_____

_____

_____

_____

_____

_____

_____

Notes n' Stuff:

_____

_____

_____

_____

_____

_____

_____

_____

_____

_____

_____

_____

_____

_____

_____

_____

_____

_____

_____

_____

_____

_____

_____

_____

Notes n' Stuff:

_____

_____

_____

_____

_____

_____

_____

_____

_____

_____

_____

_____

_____

_____

_____

_____

_____

_____

Notes n' Stuff:

_____

_____

_____

_____

_____

_____

_____

_____

_____

_____

_____

_____

_____

_____

_____

_____

_____

_____

_____

_____

Notes n' Stuff:

Notes n' Stuff:

Notes n' Stuff:

_____

_____

_____

_____

_____

_____

_____

_____

_____

_____

_____

_____

_____

_____

_____

_____

_____

_____

_____

Notes n' Stuff:

_____

_____

_____

_____

_____

_____

_____

_____

_____

_____

_____

_____

_____

_____

_____

_____

_____

_____

_____

Notes n' Stuff:

Notes n' Stuff:

_____

_____

_____

_____

_____

_____

_____

_____

_____

_____

_____

_____

_____

_____

_____

_____

_____

_____

_____

_____

_____

Notes n' Stuff:

Notes n' Stuff:

_____

_____

_____

_____

_____

_____

_____

_____

_____

_____

_____

_____

_____

_____

_____

_____

_____

_____

_____

_____

Notes n' Stuff:

_____

_____

_____

_____

_____

_____

_____

_____

_____

_____

_____

_____

_____

_____

_____

_____

_____

_____

_____

Notes n' Stuff:

_____

_____

_____

_____

_____

_____

_____

_____

_____

_____

_____

_____

_____

_____

_____

_____

_____

_____

_____

_____

_____

_____

Notes n' Stuff:

_____

_____

_____

_____

_____

_____

_____

_____

_____

_____

_____

_____

_____

_____

_____

_____

_____

_____

_____

So, what now?

I hope you've had an inspired journey over the past 90-ish days. And hey, it doesn't matter to me if it took you 90 consecutive days, or 90 sporadic days over a 6-month period. Every little bit helps, and you're much better off doing a day of reflection every few days, than never doing any days at all!

If you enjoyed using this self-love journal, and you think someone could benefit from the regular practice of counting blessings and acknowledging the good stuff, do me a favour and share this book with someone who needs it! You can snap a photo of the cover and tag me on social media (@MomfidentAF), sharing how your experience was - even the tricky parts. I would really appreciate hearing your feedback!

And listen: confidence, self-acceptance, and ultimately self-love, is an ongoing journey. Completing a 3-month self-love practice is an incredible first step, but make sure you're continuing this practice in some way as you move forward with your daily life! Aim to also teach your children, your partner, and any friend who needs it - about the importance of taking the time to focus heavily on the positive pieces of their lives.

Sending you love, light, gratitude and love,
- Courtney
XO

About the author

Courtney St Croix is a published author, Mindset Educator and Women's Confidence Coach, and has been a leader in the Canadian fitness industry for the past fourteen years. In 2015, Courtney set out on a personal journey to whole-body self-acceptance, as she recovered from the ultimate female body transformation experience of pre- and post-pregnancy.

Through a long-time struggle with a lack of both confidence and a healthy body image, Courtney wanted to figure out how to create and foster a more confident and self-assured mindset. After becoming a certified Life Coach, with specialties in Life Purpose and Confidence Coaching, she now understands where true confidence is conceived, and aims to share the truths of self-love and self-acceptance with women on a daily basis.

Courtney lives in Ontario, Canada with her husband Chris, daughter Presley and colossal dog, Molson.

For more information about Courtney, please visit GetMomfidentAF.com, find Courtney on Instagram (Instagram.com/MomfidentAF), or email hello@momfidentAF.com.

59442399R00088

Made in the USA
Middletown, DE
12 August 2019